Can You Still Feel the Butterflies?

poems by

Lindsay-Rose Dunstan

Finishing Line Press
Georgetown, Kentucky

Can You Still Feel the Butterflies?

Author's Note:

The following collection of poems draws from my own stories as a person with
lived experience, as well as some of my clients' stories. All of them have given
me permission to share their stories; for that I am deeply grateful. Portions
of "Pebbles" were previously published in *Rock Paper Poem*; and "Dancing
on Diamonds" has been published in *45 Magazine*. As a content warning,
"The Cold Outside" contains references to sexual assault; "Suicide Bimbo"
and "Jean Tatlock's Butterflies" reference suicide.

Publisher: Leah Huete de Maines
Editor: Christen Kincaid
Cover Art: Illustration by Alexa Karabin
Author Photo: Lindsay-Rose Dunstan
Cover Design: Elizabeth Maines McCleavy

Order online: www.finishinglinepress.com
              also available on amazon.com

Author inquiries and mail orders:
Finishing Line Press
PO Box 1626
Georgetown, Kentucky 40324
USA

Contents

Dedication (Or, Open Letter to God)

Dear God,
I have a few dozen queer Muslim clients,
each mistakenly believing they are alone.
One of them, at age 8, told his mom to tell You
You'd made a mistake.

You gave me ears to hear stories
and a pencil to write them—
with an eraser for the trans kid in Yemen
who knew he was a boy when he was 8
and 30 years later he came to me
to help him fix Your mistake.

This book is dedicated:
to those bold enough to call out gods on mistakes they made
to those mad enough to believe in their dreams
to those who want what they haven't seen
to those who agree that it is insane to want to fit in
to a world like this one
to those saying we don't need a world with institutions:
let's take care of each other and make a new one.

Paper Covers Rock

My sixth-grade teacher was kind enough to come up with a nickname for me, one my classmates quickly adopted. Inspired by my tendency to stare blankly into the void for long periods, he dubbed me "Space Cadet." In medical school, I learned about absence seizures, and wondered whether that was my deal back then. (It wasn't, because kids grow out of absence seizures, and my little quirk has persisted into adulthood.) When other people notice me in Space Cadet mode now, they may make more polite references to "zoning out" or "the blue screen of death." But there is a clinical word for this phenomenon: dissociation.

I tell my clients that we dissociate because it works. It's a skill that we developed so long ago we have honed it perfectly, to escape painful moments—to put things into boxes in the interests of getting shit done.

I *wish* I could feel one way about dissociation. Instead, I feel two things about it. The other way I would describe dissociation is that it's a sneaky little trap that steals us away from the *now*. That it numbs just as much joy as it does pain. That it's the reason you struggle to remember how insanely loved you felt at one time, just because so much other garbage was happening around that time.

(But I'll let you in on a happy little secret: we can practice conjuring it back up. I promise you, when you see your grandmother's face in your meditation space smiling down at you from your circle of care, you will wonder how you were ever oblivious she was there.)

Another downside to shoving your shit into boxes has to do with pressure and physics. Once box pressure reaches a certain threshold level, the wick to a meltdown is lit. To protect against this, I have been drawn to release pressure in my boxes with creative bursts; for me, that's with a pen. Then I can move on, and go back to my writing when I need to release the box pressure again. At the end of all of this, I remind myself, I'm gonna have a piece of art that says: *This is how I got through that really shitty period in my life.*

I will be brave enough to own this label today: I am a writer. Or as the French say (because in French, articles are dropped before names of vocations): *Je suis écrivaine.* (French speakers may notice I chose to ignore another strange convention of theirs, the lack of a feminine counterpart for the word "writer.") My goal in writing isn't to let shit go and forget about it—it's to create something with it, to weave it into a broader story of who I am in this ever-changing world. To find the strength and wisdom in it. The will to create something helps me open the boxes, and gets me up off the floor after I've done so.

Every adversity we face, every particle of shame we carry from the harms we afflicted when we were too desperate to see any other way out, brings two opportunities, wrapped in bows: to learn, and to create. I once attended a training workshop for a brief, peer-led trauma intervention called Narrative Exposure Therapy. In the first session, the client is asked to illustrate their life story using props from a kit: flowers, for the happiest moments; rocks for the traumatic ones; thread to connect the timeline, and to keep it in context. I can pick up a pen and paper and I can write. As we all know from the game of chance: paper covers rock.

The people I have harmed, and those who have harmed me, will never know what I learned from them. This most of all: keep going. Keep breathing. Keep writing.

Viktor Frankl's Gas

One of my favorite meditation techniques is what Lama Rod Owens calls "ancestor practice," where you settle into your meditation space and imagine your ancestors as a circle of care around you. You then seek guidance from actual biological ancestors, or anyone from any group you identify with, from whom you seek wisdom.

I'm a psychiatrist, and in one of my ancestor practices, I envisioned my lineage of learned psychiatrists circling me. The ones who spoke to me loudest were Jean Tatlock and Victor Frankl. Dr. Frankl was an expert on the Holocaust for the worst reason possible: he was there. At the camps one day he said:

You know what?
Before I hit the ovens I might as well make the best of it
so I might as well just do what I do best
just keep on keepin on
bein a psychiatrist, lettin folx
get shit off their chests
and while I'm at it, why not write a book

And he wrote a book. While he was in a concentration camp.
He called it "Man's Search for Meaning."

Now as he watched his family members getting escorted
one by one to the "crematorium"
where pellets of Zyklon B would wipe out half his family
Dr. F came up with an analogy about suffering and its relativity
(a crematorium for him might be
a Blue Lives Matter sign or a SCOTUS opinion for me)
and what he says about it hearkens back to 10th grade chemistry
that lesson you might have slept through
about states of matter and volume:
a gas assumes the shape of its container.

And he said the state of matter of suffering is a gas
and as a gas
it fills the entire space of whatever container it happens to be in.

Suffering takes up the entirety of whatever volume
your one-of-a-kind skull happens to hold
that skull is specific to one person: you

but at some point suffering will affect everyone else too
everyone out there walking around with a skull
has felt or will feel this too
there's a weird kind of beauty in that, he said.

I've boiled the art of riding the meltdown wave down to 6 simple steps.

Step one: See it. Observe the emotion.
Step two: Name it. *This is a meltdown; this is a moment of suffering.*
Boom, now there's distance between you and it.
You and your suffering are not one in the same here
but stay with me here:
Step three is to own it.
Because this experience is yours and yours alone now
I know it's scary, but it's up to you to be brave now
and move on to the next step, the one we all think we can bypass
numb it away with whatever lidocaine gets us through the day
maybe it's alcohol maybe it's workahol
maybe it's sex with all the wrong people
but whatever it is, whatever you do, how bout this: don't go there today
just go right on to
Step four: Feel it.

Feel your feels baby girl.

I know. They're out of the bottle now and it stings like a sonofabitch
but you got this and now
guess what?
You can move on to
Step 5: Let it go.
But this ain't a Disney movie baby girl.
We don't stop there
we can't magically let shit go and poof it's not there
nope, we gotta move on to

Step 6: Let it float.
Letting it float is when you remind yourself
over and over again that you have the power
to give your feelings, even the "bad" ones, space.
You can watch them expand into a potentially infinite place
dwindling, dissolving, diluting
and let me tell you, this whole process:
hurts like hell.

No one said it was easy
just that it's how you get free.
feel, baby feel that hurt, then say it with me:

Let it go.
Let it float.
Let it fill this motherfuckin' room like Victor Frankl's gas.

Let it go.
Let it float.
Let it fill this motherfuckin' room like Victor Frankl's gas.

Jean Tatlock's Butterflies

Dr. Tatlock:
queer psychiatrist who radicalized Oppenheimer
born in a world 64 years younger
I see you, your quantum paradoxes
you and me, a pair o'docs
drawn to *idées de la révolution* like moths to flames
but you got paralyzed / somehow
one too many flames for the moth
and the burnout hit so hard

constant emotion inertia—
with objects in love, we tend to stay in love
devotion paradox: blessing and curse

we call it 'emo' now, Jeannie—
how did you get through medical school without Jimmy Eat World?

the first star I see may not be a star
and this is what she said gets her through it:
"if I don't let myself be happy now then when?
if not now, when?"
the time we have now ends
when the big hand goes round again
can you still feel the butterflies?
can you still hear the last goodnight?

it's a wonder you breathed as long as you did
the same wonder that expands our chests keeps the stars apart
the wonder that made our mothers give birth
I stand on your shoulders so I can keep seeing
I stand on this boulder this rock we call earth
with my telescope view of all the light that survived
the light that keeps us alive and breathing
the light that reminds us (in every bathtub and sea) to listen to the water
listen to your sister, your mother, your daughter
pass the basket along to the other red riding hoods in pain
the little engines that could
form a train until they can reach the thread that leads them
to their own damn self, their solid home
one no big bad wolf can blow over
the reminder that this itself will blow over

because the universe requires it
(that this too shall pass)

just hold on Jeannie
just dream of me and I'll follow your thread
Jeannie dream of me to light up the courage so I can find it
so I can find you and remind you that you are a butterfly still
flapping your wings of many colors to me, to someone I mended,
who then cracked someone up—
I see the wise caterpillars who know they're not done growing
and in 64 years the dreamers will outlive me and forgive me
and be just a larva still

Go There

a client once told me they used a needle and thread to repair
a niece or nephew's teddy bear
they took the time to sew a heart in there
can you imagine a gesture more tender?
go there.

another client told me about a trip she took
to the Great Smoky Mountains of Tennessee
a single spot where you can see for hundreds of miles
a limitless view all fancy-free
but unless you're tryna be a park ranger's detainee
you have to leave by a certain time.
on a whim she decided to stay behind for just a moment
waited for the last fellow hiker to leave so she could be alone and
stood there by herself looking out at those great mountains.

just like she felt it on the top of that mountain
if you were there you would have felt it too:
all of this, for me?
yes my dear: all of this is for you
and here's the kicker: when she felt it then, it was true for her too
how can that possibly be?

the paradox only works if you can take this quirky doc's word for it
it's true because we're all connected.
there was a spark that happened when time never began
a spark that keeps firing from here into infinity
the spark opened the voltage-gated channel
that got my client's heart to beat in that very moment
from the top of a mountain in Tennessee
(a mountain that whispered to her
to change her major from urban studies
to something that would allow her to see
more *this* more of what this earth can offer her
maybe environment and wildlife? she has no idea yet)
that spark is in her, that spark is in me
and she has no idea she loaned her memory to me
as an alternate image of what being alone can be
the one with the hundreds of miles of mountains
outstretched just for me
this is what I'm afraid of?

this?

I could run away but it seems much smarter to face it
in fact run right toward it, to my fellow humans' happy places
change the channel from panic to wonder
a neuron's course can be corrected
(because you and her and me, we're all fucking connected)
so you, hey you, yeah you over there
welcome to this circle of care
just take her memory and my word for it
all of this is for you, you don't have to earn it
you have the power to shift your awareness
find happy moments, yours or shared
see the flip side of what you thought you were scared of
if you don't want to be here it's simple:
go there.

Are You There, Maude?

I remember in my 20s, low-key inwardly scoffing at folx who stopped going to mass and declared themselves "spiritual but not religious." *How is that even possible?* I wondered. In my 30s, I used to feel perplexed sitting next to fellows in 12-step meetings whose "higher power" was so clear to them, and yet was somehow not just "God." *I guess I'm a thousand times more humble than thou art,* I thought to myself, borrowing a burn from Weird Al's "Amish Paradise." *What, you think you know how to do this without a sacred book of rules to help? You think you can just see for yourself?*

Now, I'm in my 40s. I experience the divine as ancestral wisdom taking the form of a sea of radiant colors, almost cartoon-like in their brightness. My source of love and light doesn't look a thing like Jesus; if anything, They look like the strange dust that swirls in an amorphous sea of glowing bright lights, perhaps vaguely taking the shape of Angela Davis in full 'fro. (NB: It would be just as ludicrous to say God is a woman than it is to say God is a man.) My representation, I realize, is highly esoteric; I also understand now that every single member of the human race is tasked with coming up with their own version (if they want to).

I pause here to borrow one of Rory Scovel's jokes, from his special "Sex, Religion, and a Few Things in Between." He mentioned a bumper sticker on a woman's car that said, "First, God created man. Then, He had a better idea." Did *He* now? Did "He"?

She was so close, though.

As far as I can see, all organized religions and less-organized cults have male-written rules of conduct; most of them expect us to believe that the creator of the universe gives a fuck whether women are menstruating or not.

For my first dance with religion, I was unknowingly paying tithes that went to priests' lawyer fees to cover up sexual abuse. For my second dance, I enrolled in a religion whose hierarchy peaks not with one cisgender heterosexual man, but with nine of them; they believe women will be excluded from serving in these roles for at least the next one thousand years (by which time our planet will for sure be long-melted). These men live and work in Haifa, Israel, where they do not pay taxes, and live in harmony within the Israeli state. Politics (and protests) are seen as disunifying and are therefore forbidden. The floors in the 6-story building where the nine of them (and, seriously, only the 9 of them) work are covered in Pentelikon marble from Greece. Last fall, less than one hundred miles from their home, dozens of Palestinian babies died, because the Israeli government would not spare them the small amount of electricity they needed to keep incubators running.

The dead babies! I remember wanting to scream at them. But I know my cries would echo within the 58 Corinthian columns of their office entrance, and I would be met with 18 shoulders—not cold shoulders, but something far more dangerous: warm ones, shrugging in silence.

As a college student in Ann Arbor, once I got over my fear of driving on expressways, I realized I could visit my Grandma Rose anytime I wanted. (She was just about 20 minutes down I-94.) This was a real game-changer in terms of managing my stress level. I'd bust my ass in my pre-med classes, convinced I would not pass any of them if I allowed myself more than 3 or 4 hours of sleep per night. On Friday evenings, instead of going out drinking and socializing like neurotypical college students, I'd show up at Gram's with residual knots in my academic stomach, ready to get my chillax on.

We'd spend evenings watching TV in her living room; I took the armchair that had been my grandfather's throne, until he widowed my grandmother in 1987. Grandma would bring out glasses of Diet Coke (with ice cubes), and a big bowl of cheese popcorn mixed with potato chips. Just as I was comforted by my grandmother herself, she in turn seemed comforted by watching old TV shows in syndication, reminders of a simpler time.

Nick-at-Nite was eye-opening for me. I was already a fan of Bea Arthur's work from watching her in *The Golden Girls* as a child; I wasn't even aware she had starred in her own sitcom years before that. It was an *All in the Family* spinoff called *Maude*, in which Maude embodies second-wave feminism as precisely as Archie Bunker had embodied rancid conservatism. The show had a decent 6-season lifespan, but was canceled in 1978, a few months before I was born.

Nineteen years after *Maude* ended its run, I became an instant fan.

Maude lived with her fourth husband in upstate New York. The proto-Dorothy Sbornak was even sassier, wiser-cracking, and deader-pan—

and much more vocal about political topics. The show took on women's lib, civil rights, and, perhaps most famously, abortion. My devoutly Catholic grandmother's praise of that episode was a wink-wink I could cling to later in life, when I came to understand that I am under no obligation to believe or do everything a priest says I should believe or do.

####

1994:
bobbing for apples in a church basement
(Catholic youth group Halloween party)
my secret crush holds my head down in the water
(for laughs)
triumphant apple in my mouth, but my brain screams *death*
(that's what brains do when airways occlude)

1978:
priest holds my head down in water
(baptism or waterboarding?)
shows me who's boss
everyone celebrates while my brain screams death

1987:
my grandmother baptizes my cousin in her kitchen sink
holds her tenderly
lets the water say the words.

####

Are you there, Maude?

It's me, Lodes.

I'm going to breathe with you for awhile, okay?

Matter and Energy

in high school my physics teacher would have what I now know were
hangover days
and he'd feel the need to sit in the back of a dark room
rather than try to teach a bunch of redneck teens
what they had to know about the building blocks of matter.
he'd throw in a VHS tape to do his bidding and heavy lifting
and thank Maude he did, because Carl Sagan's *Cosmos* blew my mind.

a stunning late-70s graphic about the origins of life:
Vivaldi soundtrack, squiggly atoms into chromosomes
spanning from primordial soup all the way
to the cis white heterosexual man.

the line's not done squiggling.
at least as much time must remain
as the amount of time that's already past,
and what is time, anyway?
did that exist pre-bang?
take a step back.

imagine your parents in the 1960s
the first time actual photos were released
showing what Planet Earth looks like from space.
can you wrap your brain around infinite?
well, of course not, but
why don't you even bother to try?
It makes your problems, your life's largest losses
look like nothing at all.

is that why you look away?
scary to confront the what-the-hell-is-this-all-for.
might make you want to throw in the towel
embrace the hedonic
destroy what you can't take with you on your way out the door
but guess what?
the squiggly line draws another door.
you assume consciousness disappears
the moment your brain stops sparking
but tell me—where the hell does it go?
and does it have to pay for parking?
please tell me 'no' but even so:

take a step back.

there is matter,
there is energy,
there is infinity,
and that, my friend, is it.

I've been told (by 3700 case reports
of those who experienced an NDE;
near-death experiences are being scientifically studied,
rigorously enough to warrant acronym)
that the destination looks like a bright light.

when I feel paralyzed with loss and longing I tell myself
to move just one step, and make it backwards
to widen my perspective, see the grand scheme of things
the brutal beautiful truth that everyone I have loved and lost
is as tiny as a cilium
and they're just down the cell from me,
propelling an organism called 'humanity' into some general direction—

I will both let go and hold them all
hold them in the bright warm light
if you remember one thing please remember this:

the light is in me,
the light is in you.

Non-Silence

white woman writing about revolution based on love:
sounds authentic (it is)
sounds tender and true (she tries)

/ it might make you feel better
to hear another well-intended healer
equating peace with non-violence
(but it shouldn't)

if she could she would be there:
the one time she insists on being up front

/ to take bullets

if she could not take bullets she would be there:
to bear witness

we're all terminal
save me, doctor: save my life and if you can't
you bear witness

/ 61 indicted

only linked arms can save us
if you are a tree or a citizen

/ it won't make you feel better
to wax poetic about peace

without also taking down cop city

Extreme Playlist

The punchline is: my Extreme playlist is the song "More Than Words" on repeat.

The joke is, "Extreme" was a one-hit wonder who released their one hit, a monster ballad called "More Than Words," in 1991.

The joke had come to me after I misidentified both Nelson and Mr. Big in a text conversation with a 47-year-old.

The real joke is, these are all interchangeable bands of Gen-X's sordid music history.

anyway, she wants it
she built this city on rocks she threw at meaningless marriage certificates
at monsters rocking her like a hurricane
pour some sugar cane over the poison she drank
like ice cold November rain
every gun has its rose
every rose has its thorn
every thorn tells a story of some interchangeable Mr. Big
who couldn't take her high enough
to see a way out—until David Lee said jump
and the trampoline sent her up
to be shown for herself more than words
could ever say that's the way
she needs it

what was it the paramedic said?
(we're still connected by a thread)
I've seen this a hundred times, honey, and believe me
no man is worth it

waiting for us is and always will be the choice of one more breath
and we can take it
when we decide we're not gonna take it anymore

Zombie

you collect ex-lovers like charms dangling
from a hospital ID bracelet

so many charms, so many snakes and
habit energy compels you like a zombie
to men who use your body

I don't know why, you don't know why,
but are we both going to pretend this isn't what's happening?

don't let them down or they'll let you have it
they are (in)patiently waiting to be cared for again
to be carried again in their mommy's womb
gestating backwards til you're a mummy in a tomb
you won't resist

I can tell by what's hanging from your wrist

The Cold Outside

(an ekphrastic poem describing the painting "Le Verrou," by Jean-Honoré Fragonard)

A scene depicts two people entwined in a bedroom
                    baby it's cold outside
A man, disrobed to his undergarments
                    baby it's bad out there
A woman, still compressed in corset, bearing a petticoat
                    it's up to your knees out there
He stands on tippy toes to reach the bolt of the door
                    what's the sense in hurting my pride
But his calves, crafted by chisel, amply propel
                    no cabs to be had out there
Aims his lips at her face
                    gosh your lips look delicious
She pushes him away
                    think of my lifelong sorrow
Along perfect diagonal, locked bolt lines up with forbidden apple
                    get over that holdout
Dark red drapes like labia, corner of the bed thrusting triumphant in
the light
                    I'd like to think of it as opportunistic
A vase has fallen but not broken
                    that took a lot of convincing

I really can't say
                    her position ambiguous

I simply must go

        maybe she's warm inside

Say, what's in this drink

        you need a tongue to tell

So nice and warm

        how she feels to him doesn't matter

I've got to get home

        baby the door is locked

The neighbors might think

        she is about to be raped

My father will be pacing the floor

        his eyes can read the story

Maybe just a cigarette more

        maybe she needs poison

So nice and warm

        maybe she wants poison

The answer is no

        mystery solved

To be filed under: uninterpretable without audio (ekphrastic failure)

Suicide Bimbo

she deflects with humor
calls herself "suicide bimbo"
because she could never get it right.
I remember frantically tying the knot, she tells me
I was choking and struggling and
she starts laughing softly.
I'm so embarrassed.
The knot untied itself.
I just fell to the ground.

I do not laugh with her.
Instead I imagine another patient's mother years ago
the one who found her son hanging—
(a mentor told me mental illness is sometimes terminal)
(in my darkest moments I still consider myself a murderer)
but we congregate in the light
heartedness when I suggest we throw a party for
her terrible knot-tying skills, be proud
of what she learned about how moments evaporate

I tell her nothing can stop us now
from saying the painful parts out loud
and we celebrate.

To the Cashier at the Citgo Station

one day a "crazy black woman" will come in
she will rant and rave, she will make you think
she can't be brave but here's the thing:
bravery isn't what one chooses to be
it's just what one is, when one who was beaten to death
still somehow has legs
to take another step
and the next day there was another blazing hot ball of light in the east
like clockwork
so she got back up.

she has a name but you can't say it,
not yet, because right now
you just call her the excrement
of flying mammals,
right now you just call her batshit.

you'll tense up,
crunch some numbers in your head and it turns out
the $9.50 you'll earn this hour
is the same amount you'll earn the next hour
and clockwork is funny because this hour is way too long
to listen to this woman for another goddamn minute
so you'll ask the manager what to do.

his answer will be buy the book
(on Amazon so Bezos the Clown might get you a better job,
might pay you circus peanuts
minus this freakshow) you go by the book:
If a disruptive customer is not redirectable,
call 911.

but what if you knew?
911 is a mine, a stun gun, it's swine come undone, it's a fine, an un-sung
"hero without a cape" but with a firearm?
if you knew what it means to call that number
you would know those "heroes" won't save this woman,
just lock her in a cage til she can calm herself down—
they'll make a crime of her rage, they'll arrest her
for not being nice to them when they showed up.

you would know what it could mean to tap SOS
with our intertwined fingers
Samuel Morse didn't mean lethal force,
he meant we can
save our selves

so maybe you'll call a different number.
maybe you'll ask her if she has a friend she could call.
maybe she'll call a sister from AA, and if so
there's no maybe.
that sister shows up,
(she'll show up she'll show up)

with the ding of a bell about to
save and be saved
she will burst through the door
in a shirt and shoes
ready for service.

she will show up,
she will *say her name.*
she will say I'*m here now.*
she will say *and you:*
and you, my dear, you:
you are safe now.

she'll take her hand.
hands held, no hands up
(don't shoot)
(don't you see?)

it's magic

AbraCadABra!
this woman's been sawed in half
(but she's still got those legs, remember)
and now she joins with another
a nonbinary sibling, a sister, a brother
It is the purest kind of magic, I swear to you.

why call a pig
when this woman can pull a rabbit right out of her hat
(to make room for the halo)

you see it now?

angels for each other.
the only number worth calling
is nine hundred eleven miles from the nearest bullet
the only law worth enforcing
is the law of attraction
nature abhors a vacuum
but nurture adores a classroom
and you,
and you, and you, and you
you can learn now.

did you know?
scientists once randomized 22 galago monkeys
all with wounds from chronic self-injurious behavior
11 of them were prayed for
(the other 11, controlled)
the ones who were prayed for healed faster
(seriously, they measured the size of each wound
with tiny little scab-sized rulers)

it's not placebo because they weren't even human
it's not religion because it's just human kindness
it's not science because this kind of healing
is called poetry
(I know it because I wrote it after a sister loaned it)

it's how we call each other,
by our names
it's how we hold each other up
until that blazing hot ball of light pops back up in the east
like clockwork
and the big hand comes round again
to be held and not cuffed
because this time you called someone else.

Locker Room

Locker? I barely know her
and she is sometimes he and he was once a
beauty pageant winner, graduate of the finest
finishing school Mom could send her to because
she kept getting into fist fights at her
unfinishing school.

she said she knew she was queer
when he was in the locker room at school
and it felt like he was spying.
I started showing up early for swim, late for gym
just kept trying to understand who I was
I was smokin' hot but one of his bros
he said I was missing a few chick parts
I told him he'd never find those in me but he proposed
anyway and I thought "he'll do"
so she said "I do"
and the marriage lasted six months.

can't locker up, can't figure him out
she'll put on a suit and you'll start to doubt
he keeps you guessing but it's not cross dressing
it's putting clothes on a body, this body
her body, his body
a body you may have opinions about
but just shut the fuck up, lock your shit up
in your locker, remember the combination
of kindness and affirmation
drop a couple out for the gender deviations
the pronoun celebrations the endocrinology consultations
(they don't owe you an explanation)
then peace out.

Pebbles

Act I: You Can Keep It
I loaned a friend a book a few weeks before
he went to prison

[if you think it matters
how he ended up there
you won't understand poetry]

he got a line from that book
tattooed on his chest (around where Superman
had the capital S) and
I still remember what he said:

your superpower is knowing what people need
to hear then not saying it

Act II: You Can Let it Go
we write to let go
(little by little)

we write to break free
(not with a grenade but a pickaxe)

our words like pebbles falling—
slipping out of Andy Dufresne's pants

our words like vines growing—
from soil sifted from gravel spoilage
our soul lifted from razed ruins

our words, not waste but refuse
refusing to look away but also looking
up up up.

Dancing on Diamonds

break-ups don't always make me think about dying
but they always make me think about dying alone
40 years later /undiscovered by neighbors
until they can hear my cats screaming
we're out of meat, meow, no more mommy meat

several hours and 9 days after I got the courage to run away
I canceled an ex's ticket to our planned vacay
to Myrtle Beach—but I went anyway
for a run on the beach around sunset
and in a whimsical seize-the-day moment
I closed my eyes and ran blindly, arms wide open
trusting the ground below me and when I opened
my eyes I was looking directly across the Atlantic Ocean

I felt myself running to another version of myself,
who in turn was running on the beach
directly across the ocean from me
my racemic enantiomer, along the same latitude
my mirror image racing to me from so far away
but sure as shit I could hear her:

bring it in, bring it in, I heard her say (I realize she wants to hold me)
breathe, I heard her say (didn't realize I'd been holding it)

a glorious exhale emptied my lungs
and my soul-sister huffed CPR across the ocean
one single continuous breath along 34 degrees north

looked it up later—the city directly across the ocean from Myrtle Beach
(found out it's Casablanca)

I heard her whispered words making ocean sounds
felt her cheek against mine: I know, I know

there, there, I'm here, I'm here
pull it together, girl, your hemisphere needs you

yet someday my hemisphere will stop needing me
and when they do, who will be at my side?

some of my proudest moments in medicine
could be interpreted in retrospect
as unconscious self-centered good karma coins
in my creepy Kevorkian death-with-dignity bank
(back then I had so much to fear)

as a trainee I would incur senior residents' wrath
when a patient of mine wanted to choose where they died
and the unit social worker, burned out to a crisp,
was nowhere to be found
I would eschew tasks for my still-kickin' patients
to make it happen for the almost-dead
get them to heaven by moving earth if I had to

got a critically ill Dominican on a plane once
one-way ticket to Santo Domingo so he could die where he lived
I could not speak to him with my limited Spanish
so to express my fondness for him I told him he was *como un gatito*
because I knew the Spanish word for kitten

later, a cancer-ridden meat-sack named Severin
old grizzled Navy veteran with no one left
no friends, no family, almost no time
he'd scream at nurses, physical therapists, specialists to leave him alone

all I did was listen
so I got to stay

but the price of admission was feeling his sadness as I left
evaporated like hand sanitizer as I walked out his door
every time

80-hour work-weeks and I remember visiting him on my day off
bringing him a lemon ice because it reminded him of being a kid
1920s Brooklyn
and tasted sweeter than nothing-by-mouth
(what the nurses didn't know wouldn't hurt him)

it took a shit-ton of phone calls but
I got him to a hospice where he could go outside
a few times before he died
(senior resident shakes his head again)

this last break-up, as my mind spiraled to my dying alone
I saw myself at Severin's Sunday bedside
and thought *maybe when it's my time, I'll have someone there like me*

then thought *oh yes, she will be very much like me*

let's say there was no prince charming
just Cinderella, rising from ashes
to ashes, dust to dust
sand melts down to glass and makes a mirror
(no one has the other shoe except her own damn self
holding up a looking glass slipper from Casablanca)

nevermind my kid's question
(*how does a shoe that fits perfectly fall off a foot*)
what I want to know is:
how does she dance with shoes made of glass
without slicing her soles to butchered feet meat

(the soul is protected / nothing to fear)

glass slippers are crafted from sand
(before it melts into reflective surface)
that's why the ocean is my ballroom
I dance on diamonds like shoeless joe's trajectory from first base
to home

score

all the single ladies with diamonds at their feet
but none on their fingers:
nothing to fear anymore

my Casablanca cousin will step in like I did for Severin
whisk me away on a staycation from myself
whisper to me as I follow the light:
here's lookin' at you, kid

and we'll take care of your cats, don't you worry

nothing to fear anymore

Pyramid

I
am
building
you a pyramid
somewhere Napoleon's
cannons can't reach their short arms;
I am your Casablanca twin cousin, I am Josephine,
I am the queen of two months of no nicotine; I am carried
in the arms of a cheerleader squad, I have arms for them now, all
the facebook friends I went to high school with who liked the diet culture
poem I posted, the women I've falsely claimed to have nothing in common with; they
are the green hands holding us up, staying glued together; look closer at the yellow and blue
atoms, drops of food coloring in a glass of water, floating around and taking it over; we can keep
ourselves safe from others and stay in our bubbles, as long as we hang out in oil! but the problem is I'm
always so curious what the rest of the world looks like—in fact it looks a lot like New York, in that I wanna be
a part of it, with my pom-poms maize and blue, start spreading the news! I have arms for them and for me, too.

The darkness that's inside her makes her feel so small, but call me Cyndi because I see her true colors shining through; look closer, at the space between black and white, within which lie the only waves in motion that human beings can perceive, and if you keep zooming in you'll just see particles spinning, and I am of the opinion they look like linked arms, singing like U can 2: *carry each other, carry each other,* yes I see her true colors, the linked arms of every Roy G. Biv and every electron spinning round and round in orbit; she herself is part of the whole, a whole particle in motion / whatever emotion she's feeling, there's a counterpart in Casablanca spinning and spinning too, reminding her across the ocean: *here's looking at you, I forgive you and whatever happens, you're a sphere and I'm still here, feeling the pull of you.*

Silica Gel

it has one simple rule:
do not eat

/famine
in line for hours to get a bag of flour
silica gel genocide says—do not eat
Palestinians say—*we are starving*
the trucks crushing their bones say—we speak louder

/religious fast
men in power, having received torches passed by
men in power who in turn received their torches from
men in power believing themselves to be God's megaphone
silica gel fast says—do not eat
instinct says—*find a source of water*
religion says—connect with God instead; exception:
I'm menstruating
religion says you're off the hook
but you're on your own

/hunger strike
scribbled oval labeled 'uncommitted'
voter in primary says—*I don't know*
(she knows damn well) (the alternative is unthinkable)
there are options, including some guy named Joe, she picks 'nah'
(hoping he will hear her)
like a hunger striker at the Golden Corral
binging on autonomy
(because she can, for now)
to have a choice is to have power
to say—*I can take it or leave it*
not in a 'meh' way—
a way that says—*thank Maude, thank Maude*

religion says—the state says—
silica gel says—Simon says—
do not eat
I say—now hear this:
I decide what goes in my body and when
whether you hear me or not—
here I am

Starvation by Summertime

I've just read the UN's horrible horoscope
about the impending holocaust in the "holy land"
(an estimated 1.1 million will be dead from starvation by summertime)

in my ancestor meditation practice space I ask Sharoug,
my long-dead Armenian great-grandmother,
who (one century ago) survived an eerily similar genocide:
what's to be done about the Palestine question?

my mom has told me random things about her
like the weird way she pronounced the word "potato"—PO-tato
so we'd sing *you say potato, I say PO-tato* and laugh and laugh—
meanwhile it's famine in Ireland and hot potatoes be droppin like flies
droppin like all the starving Palestinian kids about to die—

I line up my telescope with my neighbor's
to seek what I need to look forward
(clarity)

as I feel for lost souls leaning up against microscopes behind me
(may their plight disappear and also never get too small for me to see)

may gravity make wrecking balls out of dropped hot potatoes
may they leave cracks in the pavement so light can slip through—
may they crap their dandelion DNA into every sidewalk on every block
(how else could a flower grow between two rocks?)

what happens in the space between is magic
the synapse where dopamine wrecks its havoc
in pleasure, in pain, in times of abundance, times of need
if you listen you'll hear crickets singing and vines floating in the void
where telescope meets microscope:

colliding scopes, mirrors in a kaleidoscope
my mama likes to quote Obama: may Justice arrive like a thunderbolt

I'll close my eyes and dream of the feasting and dancing in Palestine
right here, right now, where our visions collide and our language
(if we bother to use it)
won't have a word for genocide
and there's only one way to pronounce PO-tato

and when we drop a hot one, it dances like a Mad Man off a skyscraper
in optimistic descent
(he has to believe it, I have to believe it):

so far, so good
so far, so good

With Thanks

I would like to thank my clients for sharing their stories, and my sons (David and Adam) for giving me reasons to write them down.

I would like to thank my dad for being the voice of reason through any storm, and my mom for being the reason I ever started writing in the first place.

I would like to thank my friends who graciously accepted beta-versions of these pieces in their inboxes over the years (especially Zak Saruna), and my Friends at the Detroit Friends Meeting, for their silence and non-silence alike.

I would like to thank my therapist (Emerson Delacroix) for helping me figure some of this shit out, even as I resisted.

Finally, I would like to thank my brain for being able to generate and notice my breath, over and over, for as long as it takes; and my Casablanca twin cousin for giving me spiritual CPR when I forget what to do.

Lindsay-Rose Dunstan, MD, MPH (she/they) is a freelance writer, prison/police abolitionist, and anti-carceral psychiatrist catering to those with neurodivergent conditions and marginalized identities. Dr. Dunstan has a bachelor's degree in French and francophone literature, a master's degree in health behavior and health education, and a medical degree, all from the University of Michigan. Subsequently she completed her residency training at Columbia University, followed by fellowships in public psychiatry and psychosocial rehabilitation. Her work has been published in leftist and mental health journals, poetry anthologies, and *Slate Magazine*. She has also performed in NPR's *The Moth StorySlam* and other spoken-word events. Dr. Dunstan is the author of *Growth Anatomy: An Atlas on Self-Love*, available through Intersectional Press.